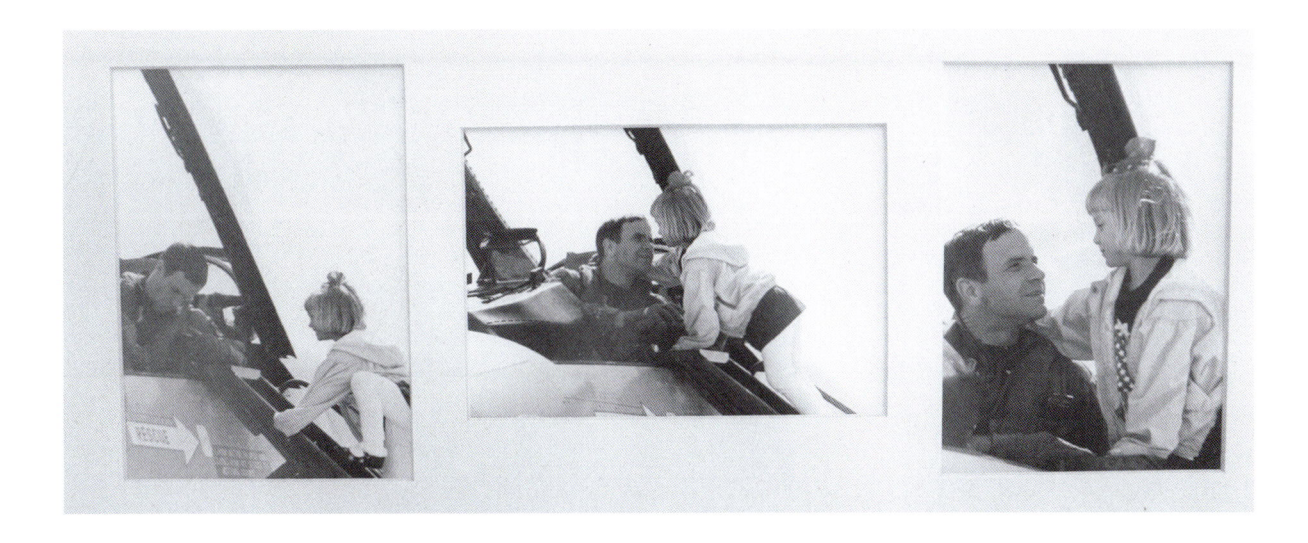

Dedicated in loving memory to my Dad, Lt. Col Mike "Mad Dog" Daniels for always keeping your promises and showing me how to live. You are deeply missed.

Published May 2019 by Wandering Roots Publishing, LLC

Copyright 2019 by Cathryn Perry.
All right reserved. No part of this publication may be reproduced of transmitted in any form or by any means, electronic or mechanical, including photocopy recording, or any information storage and retrieval systen, without permission in writing from the copyright owner.

ISBN: 978-1-951049-00-3

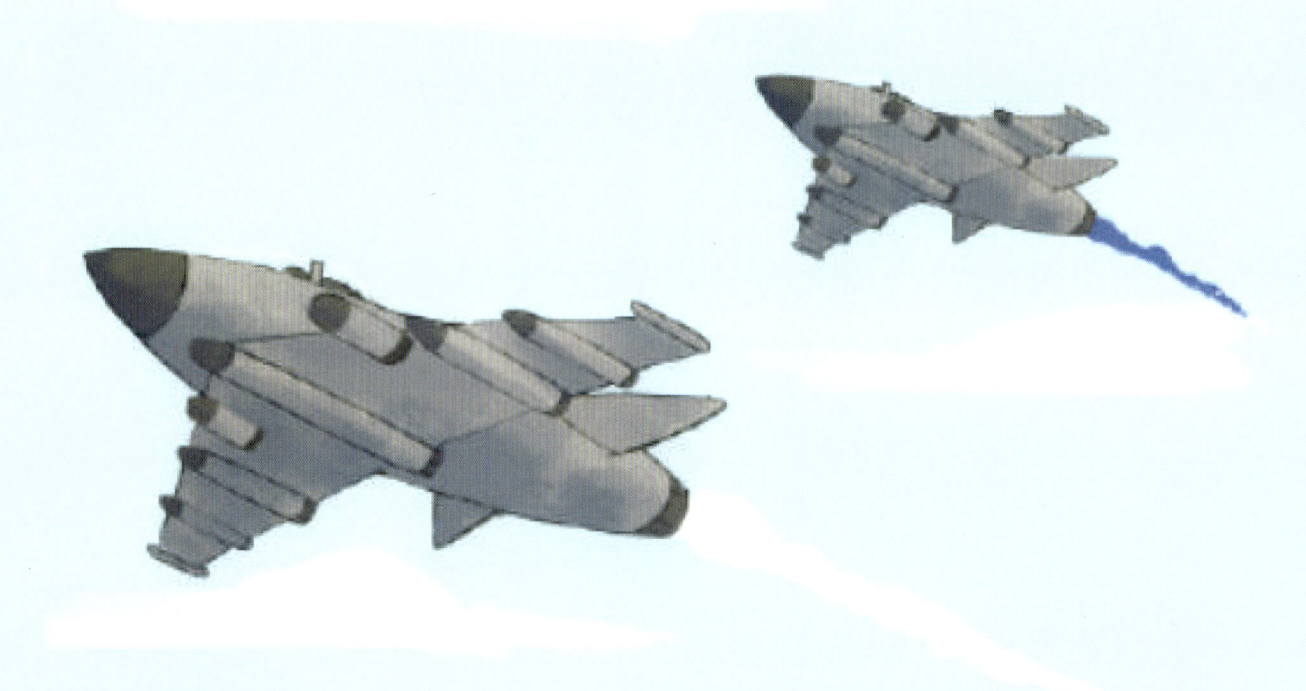

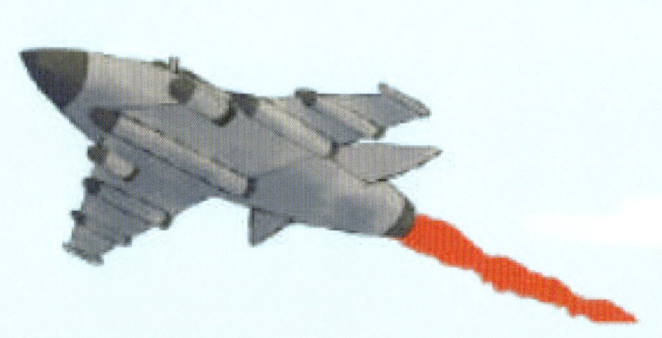

# Little Bug's Dad goes on DEPLOYMENT

Words By
Cathryn Perry

Illustrations By
Dale Zamora

The sun is shining,
little Bug is at play.
Mom and Dad call to her,
"Time to eat, come in for the day!"

Little bug ran in, and she took a seat,
Daddy bug had something to say.
What could it be? Bug pondered,
"Why was Dad so serious today?"

Daddy Bug sighed and said,
"My work needs me to fly far away.
When my job is done, I will be home,
but you will miss me for many days."

Little Bug cried, and wished him to stay,
"Can't they send another Daddy Bug
to this job far away?"

"It's always hard to leave you, little Bug.
But I must do what is right.
I have a promise to keep,
to protect you through the night."

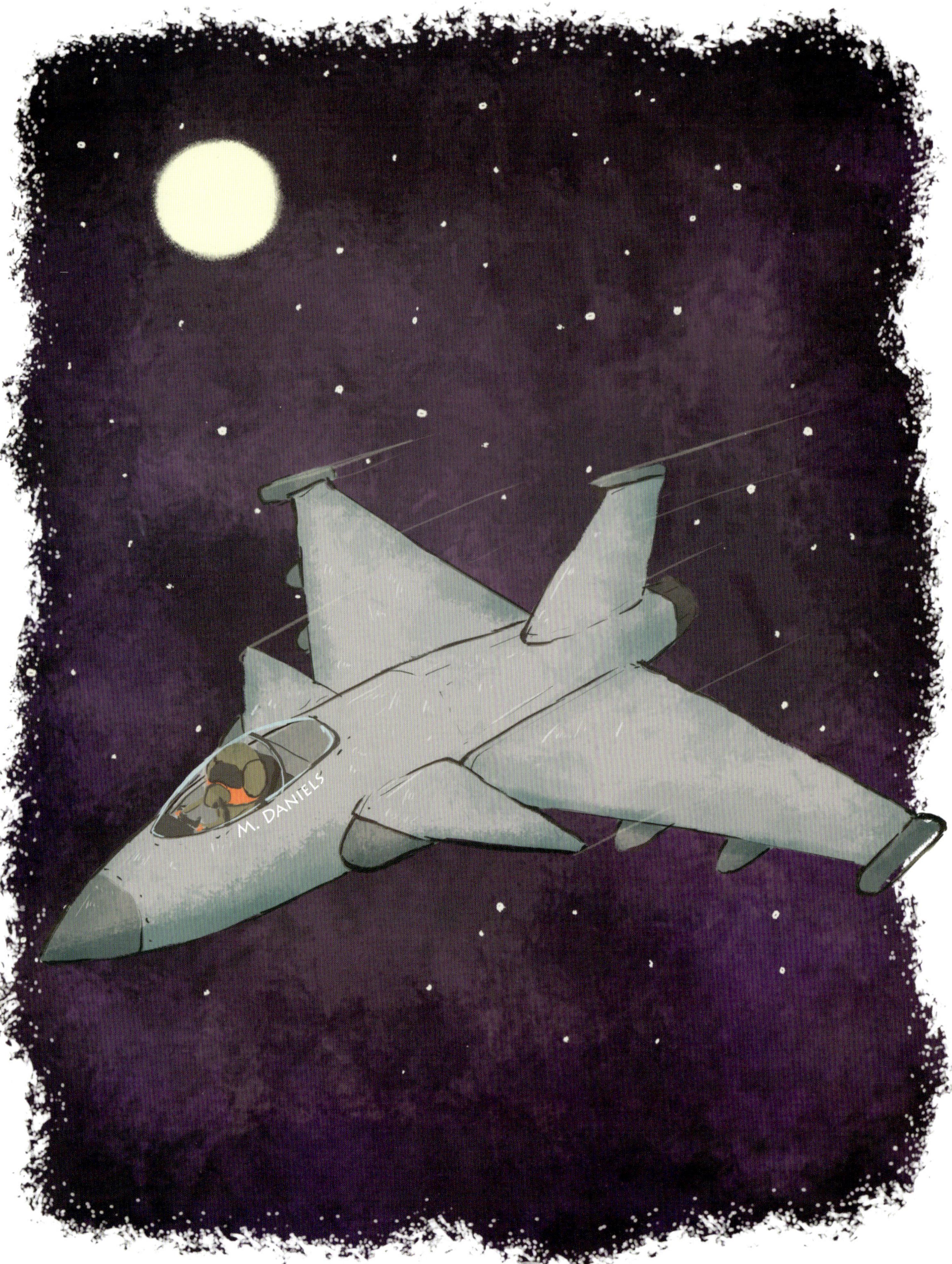
M. DANIELS

**Off he took, away he flew,
to a far off place, only he knew.
Breathing deep, his mind was clear,
Thinking of little Bug, danger drew near.**

**The fire did fly,
and the fighter fliers did fight!
All around the desert,
and all through the night.**

The fighters were tired,
but their mission was not done.
The fight isn't over men!
Not until we've won!

The fighters were done,
the battle came to an end!
Time for the fighters to land,
and take time to mend.

The mission was a success! The fighter fliers were glad!

Ready to return to their families, for GOOD had won over BAD!

At home, little Bug was dreaming of him.
So hard, she wished for her Dad.
She was ready to go play and go fish,
There were good times to be had!

1. Big hug and kiss
2. Play soccer
3. Go fishing
4. make cookies
5. show him my owie
6. more hugs

**Little Bug thought of fun and tough moments,**
**She sat and made a big list!**
**Of adventures they could have together,**
**and the challenges he missed.**

The day had come,
the base was a buzz!

Flags flew!
Engines roared,
Everyone cheered because…

# HERE THEY COME!!

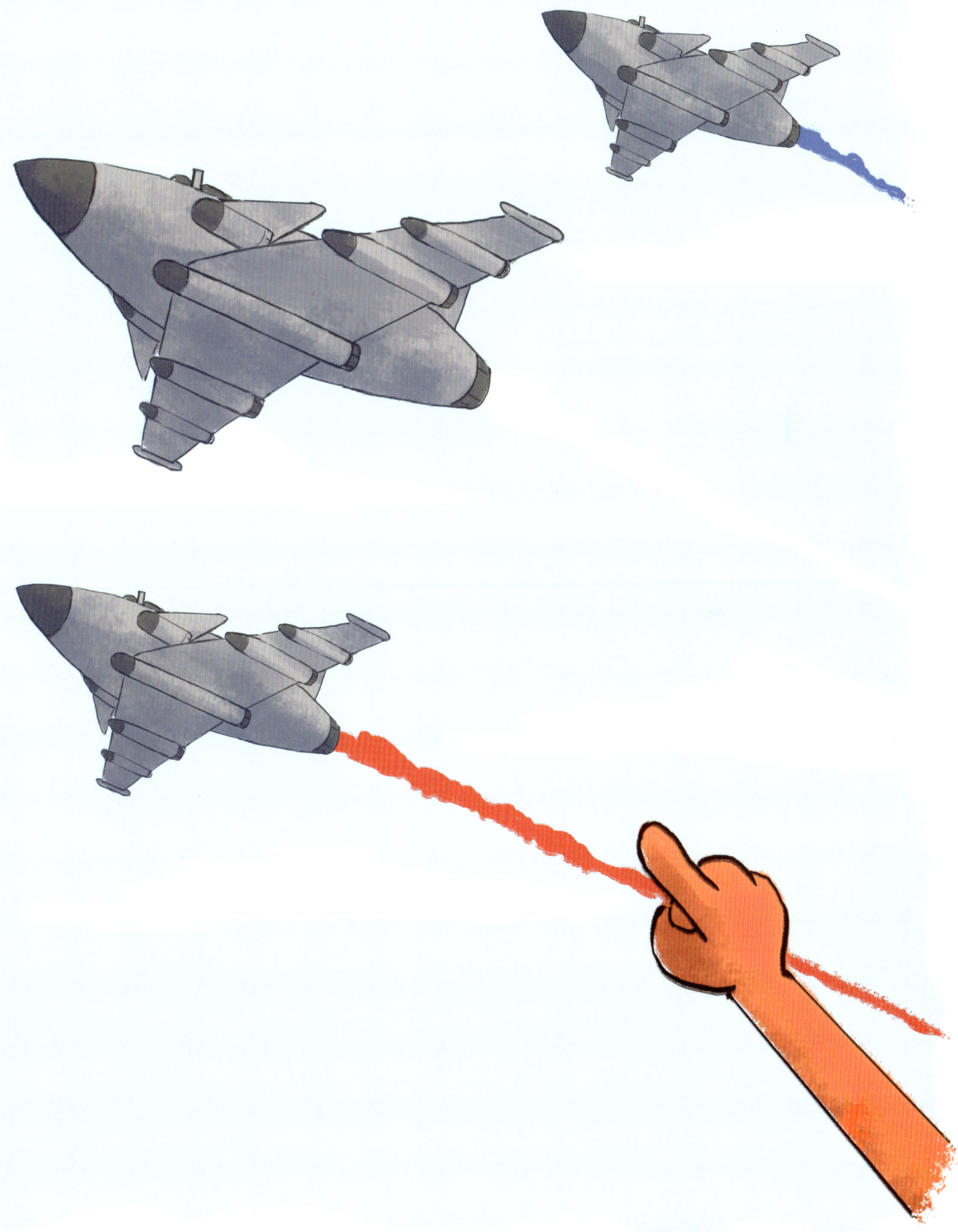

The fighter fliers landed!
The families all gathered 'round,
little Bug could NOT wait
to have her Dad on the GROUND!

Though she was small,
through the crowd she did twist!
NOTHING could stop her
from that Daddy she missed!

**Up the ladder she climbed,
almost jumped in his lap!
Wrapped her arms around him tight
and exclaimed...**

**"I'M SO GLAD YOU'RE BACK!"**

Her Daddy held her hand and said,
"I made a promise that means I must go.
But please remember, Little Bug,
I always do my best to come home."

Little bug was tucked in twice that night,
She got Dad's goodnight hug!
Her hero, her Daddy, was home now to say....

"Goodnight, Little Bug."

1. ~~Big hug and~~ kiss
2. Play soccer
3. Go fishing
4. Make cookies
5. Show ~~my~~ ...
6. m...

# The End

Thank you for supporting my book and military families around the world.

A percentage of yearly profits made from this book, Little Bug's Dad Goes on Deployment, goes to the National Military Family Association in support of military kids and their parents.

Please visit www.wanderingrootspublishing.com and cathrynperrybooks.com for FREE coloring pages, lesson plan and a deployment workbook! Or just scan the QR code below!